THROUGH WINDOWS

✛

Susan Purr

FUTURECYCLE PRESS

www.futurecycle.org

Cover photo by Ziga Radsel; author photo by Studio Emiko Photography; cover and interior book design by Diane Kistner; Caladea text and Futura titling

Published by FutureCycle Press
Athens, Georgia, USA

ISBN 978-1-942371-67-0

For Stuart, my light
for Morgan, my fire

and for Bauke who always believed

Contents

Early

Something in the way the sun rises on the Sabi
teasing purple from the hippos
eyes sleepy, they peek into the glow of morning
growing themselves from water
from the belly of a laugh

I watched from the cottage
till booms of humor from those mouths
lifted light higher through violets along the banks
where crocs waited, warming themselves in the coming gold
just in time for a punch line

I would never get the joke
yet nervously pretend to

Vulture

Atop the house, he perched
searching for sermons
bald eyes on the streets below
in shadows of faith

He would find peace among angels
claiming the lost and cleaning their feet
with bone-white love

He called for death
humble head hung low
black robes, his hunch

offering nothing to souls
but a chance to fly

Losing patience

Where does patience go
hidden deep in shadow

My failing eyes
cluttered by closets
I remember the overflowing junk drawer
in the kitchen
where everything lands eventually
paperclips conjoined in endless chains
that may be useful tomorrow
keeping all the emptiness together

I move slowly about the house
tender foot and purple
surrendering to ghosts of Legos
their built screams beneath the chairs
careless corners and unsubtle edges
tattooed with knives
ready for my close-up

Through these windows, sunshine has limits
fuzzy outlines but no face
and people watching themselves
take little notice of me in their photos
struggling with tears too big to swallow
so I squint
a lame charade of calm water
hating the flow of it

unable to forgive
the perpetual loss

Aftermath

The aftermath
grass full of purple
petals and leaves

The myrtle withstood
by letting go

through hurricane winds
long-limbed and
naked as love

Stellar

Too blind
for details

I fail to tell
between ash
and elm

where sky
touches sea
or how to get there

but I know fire

and that you are a star
fallen

The laughter gone

What about the laughter
gone
when Robin died and demons found us
vulnerable that night

He knew their names washed down with booze
leaving us guessing
Some truths are undigestible
the way we never really saw him

confessed in an empty glass
reflecting the camera lens inside-out
our failure on display
and we kept drinking
for so many years
only now a recognition
of his pain
a sleeplessness creeping of ghosts
telling yesterday's jokes

we want to laugh
with him
but the delivery tastes terrible

Bone-deep

Early risers, my uncle and I
before the sun could shake off the scales
of last night's clouds
outside the beach house

the bone-deep sea within us
we looked out upon rows of shark-tooth waves
gnashing the beach
into the guts of the world

that old fisherman told me of instinctive weather
prepping crab pots, drinking tea salted
with anecdotes

With a loaded boat, we rowed
beyond leviathans and trawling nets
to where he knew
the crabs would go

Our blood flowing over fishbones
we cast our lines
to taste the night's repast
before gull cries awakened the day

the old fisherman's smile
rivaled the dawn

Rocks in the river

So many stones
smoothed by
the cold flow of water

pants rolled above
my freezing feet

Had I seen
I would have felt
less clearly

Total eclipse—a glimpse

There was me in Cullowhee on eclipse day
ready not to see my life change
in a farmhouse rocking chair
No stranger to blindness
I sat with stupid glasses and a frowning sun

With a sudden hush, it started
cutting off the harsh cicada talk
letting crickets have a say
their softer songs for shadows
stolen heat from summer skin
My focus fell from blue
into the sea, down deep
toward my feeling space

a gentle touch, where birds nested
as light extinguished
feathers pressed reset
My glasses gone, I saw
the way out—I saw
pain and loss, forgotten—I saw
hate and worry, letting go—I saw
division and its poisons pushed aside for a glimpse
of harmony
night inside the day, cool fire and respiration

I inhaled with millions
and, somehow, we all managed to breathe

Mastery

Cats' eyes have mastered
innocence

and their turned backs
ignorance
presenting me
with ghosts

fragmented figments
of a broken vase

Blood thoughts

This is my memory bleeding
a squirrel shot by my brother
not yet dead, left for me
heavy rock in my hands
beating
until the innocence was gone

as Charlotte bleeds too
the colors of pavement and paint lit by sirens
where discrimination is squirrel-brain gray
and I can't wash it from their clothes
the rocks in my hands
beating

so much blood and no soap
I check my chest for holes
my muzzled mouth for teeth
desperate to change
the way a blind girl sees the world

understanding her fingers
clinging to tree bark
on a warm sunny day

Race

What calls to me
is blood

pounding
in your chest
beloved

and on these streets
a stain untouched
by birdsong

Living fire

Hip-hop timing snaps
I hardly noticed minutes passing
till the dancer hit her final pose
a puff of smoke

I was on my feet
but her legs kept dancing
living fire that engulfed the world
sweaty smiles and ponytails

Born to move in flashbulbs
praised for days, her long lines
genetics
and hunger beyond my reach

She can pull rhythm from the air
to spread around our house
down streets, through shops
stirring
great-grandma's embers

A history still hot
on stage with Will Rogers, kicking her gams
decades of cigarettes
and ashes
she left us

Old jazz with new blood
feathered hair and more alive in every song
scorching time
till all the music snuffs out

Sea horses

I remember seeing faces
they haunt me on a rocky shore
wide smiles and the wind in their hair
just out of reach
These spurs of clouds hurt more than metal
as the will succumbs

The need for freedom can be crushed
by froth from a maddening sea
superseded by the safety of soft words
storms seem further away

This is how you tame sea horses

My broken stride
aches in my eyes, I remember sunlight
dancing over the backs of waves
I thought I could shine with its timelessness
heels digging in to savor every image
scattering into greens and blues and browns
among the sea glass of my rods and cones

so many treasures
I must fight to find again
I remember the horse-eyed moon
unafraid of the bonfire, tasting salt air
I want to be there walking in darkness
undaunted and untamed

I want to be the words let loose
the words that will recover me

Before the leaves

Stepping out
into the open arms
of autumn

frosted kisses
on my skin
I shiver

and change color
before the leaves

Unblinking eye

The kiss burned
all that we could have said
lost in the fierceness of our mouths

crisp orange and nutmeg breaths
intending frost
within a storm of dry leaves
and veined wings
dragon weather

We pressed the fallen trees
bones of beasts and broken teeth
in ancient rings, we held so little
Promises tangled in hair are messier
when moaned

meeting the stare
of an unblinking eye

Sodden earth

I had never seen its like before
the dead bird on the side of the road
brown and black patterns, some patches of white
unmarred by death and oddly beautiful
wings outstretched
as if it had more places to go

I let it be for crows and vultures
yet it lay untouched for three days
without even so much as the eyes removed

Three days and no funeral
no resurrection, no grave

Three days
and no one would claim him
lonely in this foreign land
for all its difference, afraid
he was different

his unknown life discarded
in piles of blindness
amassing decay beyond our windows
so many strangers, falling
all over the news

I wrapped his body
front-page refugees, rescuing
careful of his wings
that still had places to go
and songs to sing

Beneath an old oak, I laid him
in sodden earth with leaves and soft goodbyes
of brown and black patterns, some patches
of white
to feel more like home

Dreamcatcher

I weave willow
for dreams
a tightly twisted halo

blessing sleep
with feathered kisses
as you stir

what wickedness
I keep for myself

Da Vinci's hands

Upon my belly masterpiece
betadine and dark red painted
ready for the artist's blades

Sharp angles touching deeper
than any man could cut
melodramas of love and wounds
removed a tumorous womb
that bloomed once a single rose
who still calls me lovely
though sewn with scars and empty spaces

Echoes and pain
a woman's cry for water
in beautiful swollen skin
destined to dimple with cracks
in cruel colors of time and so many worries

When I woke
I thought I heard da Vinci's hands clap
a work of genius
but I remember
nothing

Called west

I trekked hard
among the mountains

called west
by snaked rivers
a chance to drink
and forget it all

coiling days
around my hands
yet to let go

Vikings

New wood creaked
echoes of my hallway heels admiring
the thought of long ships
and a rolling sea

the workman paused to read me
Cap in hand, he told me tales
Ukrainian kings were once Vikings
Sanding roughness from his voice
he summoned seabirds from the sawdust
circling, they flew away

touches of stain upon his face
mostly dry
I smelled the acrid air, lost
in fumes of awkward silence

but for the faintest curl
so salty
on his lip

Caught by my laughter
his smile rose
and broke over me

Iron gates

You took me to see the old cemetery
behind a church four times older than my country
stones full of history and love
the busy birds above us
sang away time

You read names aloud
as if each one was mine
hushed but not sad
I was at peace rolling joyfully
ten thousand wildflowers
and your gentle touch of spring

I forgetting homesickness
as I was home
down a path
through iron gates
beyond roads bustling with loss

My feet would leave with you
but not my breath

Climate change

We cannot speak
from our hearts

with bullets hollowing
chests

all reason
bleeds out
whatever color
hurts the most

Souvenir from Titicaca

Despite weak sight, my legs kept climbing
up to the lake atop the world
an eye so blue, my tears rushed to it
as exiles returning from eternity abroad

But there within me, starved of breath
I bled
and though my body left that place
my vision stayed
transfixed for months beneath red clouds

By memory, a mind can see
llamas, chola hats, a sloth
faces carved in ancient rocks
the mountainside brought down to me

Draining, as the lake would do
all my dreams bleed only blue

Atlas

I would have tripped
had he not picked up my world
shaking it of dust
my first reminder

eye to eye with a black-haired dare
fierce in the lusts of rut
He turned over possibility

I asked myself who I thought I was
to horns and hooves
and two sharp snorts

the grass
the ground
while I was too busy
searching the sky

Ketchup

I sat transfixed in shadow
as a raven squeezed
a ketchup packet

fast food red on black
He stared back, satisfied
devouring my questions

so that now I truly know
everything

Rain flowers

Late-summer storms drench
flowers, all these immigrants
weeping inside me

Hunger for light

Cicada sunset
trapped in spider webs
bleeding a long summer
into silence

it sank slowly
knowing my eyes
had seized upon
the moment

devouring it
with insatiable hunger
for light

In these bones

So many poems
in these bones
I wonder

what the worms
will think
(can they?)

and would you know me
better
should they read

Borders

I like the way
pieces move
through my ocean days

dragging shapes
I almost see it all

yet my borders
remain perversely
unknown

About FutureCycle Press

FutureCycle Press is dedicated to publishing lasting English-language poetry books, chapbooks, and anthologies in both print-on-demand and Kindle ebook formats. Founded in 2007 by long-time independent editor/publishers and partners Diane Kistner and Robert S. King, the press incorporated as a nonprofit in 2012. A number of our editors are distinguished poets and writers in their own right, and we have been actively involved in the small press movement going back to the early seventies.

The FutureCycle Poetry Book Prize and honorarium is awarded annually for the best full-length volume of poetry we publish in a calendar year. Introduced in 2013, our Good Works projects are anthologies devoted to issues of universal significance, with all proceeds donated to a related worthy cause. Our Selected Poems series highlights contemporary poets with a substantial body of work to their credit; with this series we strive to resurrect work that has had limited distribution and is now out of print.

We are dedicated to giving all of the authors we publish the care their work deserves, making our catalog of titles the most diverse and distinguished it can be, and paying forward any earnings to fund more great books.

We've learned a few things about independent publishing over the years. We've also evolved a unique, resilient publishing model that allows us to focus mainly on vetting and preserving for posterity poetry collections of exceptional quality without becoming overwhelmed with bookkeeping and mailing, fundraising activities, or taxing editorial and production "bubbles." To find out more about what we are doing, come see us at www.futurecycle.org.

www.ingramcontent.com/pod-product-compliance
Lightning Source LLC
Chambersburg PA
CBHW060045050426
42448CB00012B/3126